A Remembrance

Lj Orten

authorHOUSE®

AuthorHouse™
1663 Liberty Drive
Bloomington, IN 47403
www.authorhouse.com
Phone: 1 (800) 839-8640

This is a work of fiction. All of the characters, names, incidents,
organizations, and dialogue in this novel are either the products
of the author's imagination or are used fictitiously.

Published by AuthorHouse 11/05/2018

ISBN: 978-1-5462-6553-5 (sc)
ISBN: 978-1-5462-6552-8 (e)

Print information available on the last page.

Any people depicted in stock imagery provided by Getty Images are models,
and such images are being used for illustrative purposes only.
Certain stock imagery © Getty Images.

This book is printed on acid-free paper.

Because of the dynamic nature of the Internet, any web addresses or
links contained in this book may have changed since publication and
may no longer be valid. The views expressed in this work are solely those
of the author and do not necessarily reflect the views of the publisher,
and the publisher hereby disclaims any responsibility for them.

Scripture quotations marked MSG are taken from THE MESSAGE.
Copyright © 1993, 1994, 1995, 1996, 2000, 2001, 2002, 2003 by Eugene
H. Peterson. Used by permission of NavPress Publishing Group. Website.

Contents

As is typical of Great Northwest coastal towns in America, people don't necessarily wander through them. No, they are usually drawn as if by some huge invisible magnet. A young musician and her unseen audience experience, in audible tones, a moment in time that could forever change a detour from the past. This is your invitation to a remembrance and insight into God's heart.

A young musician enters the town, and in descriptive form literally brings to life a portion of Psalm 49:4 "I WILL BREAK OPEN MYSTERIES WITH MY MUSIC, AND MY SONG WILL RELEASE RIDDLES SOLVED"

BroadStreet publishing group; Stairway Ministries, TPT

Introduction

This story is about many different stories. My intent was to highlight some experiences people have had regarding the church. There are radically divergent views about the function of the Christian Church, not to mention doctrinal differences, worship experiences and lifestyles. However, something occurred to me in my conversations with people who claim to believe in God but would never darken the door of a church building after some negative interactions had taken place. I began to see a common denominator in dialogue's I've had with these same individuals. It seems that in every instance these people had an event or experience where they came to a sudden halt in their spiritual walk. While their pilgrimage continued, it was more of the same. The old saying, two steps forward and on step back was a recurring theme. Somewhere along the way we get stuck. Whatever incident started the process of walking in circles, needed to be addressed. In an attempt to alleviate this distress a story began to emerge. The very same thing happened to me, and for several years whenever anything would go wrong, it was like I was transported back to this single event. I would feel all kinds of negative emotions and wonder if it would ever end. Then one day a sort of miraculous thing happened. After praying for years about it I realized the *thing* was gone. I thought about the place, and the events and felt nothing! I even tried to dredge up some of the old feelings and they were simply gone. The Bible does mention that old things are passed away and all things become new when we become new creations in Christ. **Colossians 3:1—11** states "For you have acquired new creation life which is continually being renewed into the likeness of the one who created you; giving you the full revelation of god. In this new creation life, your nationality makes no difference, or your ethnicity, or economic status—they matter nothing. For it is Christ that means everything as He lives in every one of us!" (The Passion translation) May I take artistic license and add gender identity to that list? After all, this is a work of fiction, which of course always has threads of real-life experience thrown in. I would like to point out that while this is a work of fiction, the events mentioned here are illustrations of illumination, meant to entertain and at the same time possibly, inject the predicament of humanity in dealing with problems, or misunderstandings with a dose of God conversation. We are, simply put, unable to figure it all out. Sometimes the Spirit just steps in, and we can receive from a higher authority, whatever we need. The question remains, do we dare believe that the Lord of the heaven's cares about us personally? I believe the Spirit does speak in a number of ways, and this story is an attempt to illustrate that possibility. So, I invite you to passenger with me on this journey and discover for yourself where it is you are going, while listening to the sounds of a song written just for you.

Chapter 1

The Girl Who Plays Guitar

There was a rugged mystical feeling about this particular west coast town. The young woman noticed that it appeared more like a small city. She stopped to breathe in the aromas and feel the essence of her surroundings. One moment the sky would be gray and moody, and then without warning a biting cold wind would grab the elements, flinging them away to reveal a bright blue splash overhead. Then, just as the sun would peek through, some sulfur looking mist would descend, wrapping a shroud of cold around the entire town. The personality of the place drew the young musician in. This is where she would stay.

During the writing of her songs the girl visited quiet places; however, it was becoming increasingly difficult to find the solitude she needed to recreate the sound she heard in the night. It was on one of her many walks, that one day she came upon a rundown church on a side street. This would be her concert hall. She didn't know it yet, but divine intervention was about to intrude into not only her life, but into the lives of those passing by.

They would hear what would seem like an assault from the past, to bring healing and resolution to the present.

A tall woman descended the concrete steps. It was getting dark and she was anxious to find her way home, and rest from the day. The introduction came as she bounded off the landing to the sidewalk below. She literally stumbled into the young woman carrying what appeared to be a guitar case. Her long reddish hair hung over one eye as she looked up in surprise. "Hi" spoke the pastor, "I'm Jill". The girl stumbled over her words apologizing for her ineptness, "oh, nice to meet you. My name's Jack. Sorry, I didn't see you. It's getting dark and I don't see well in the dark." Jill responded with a wry smile. "Well Jack, it's nice to meet you. You have an unusual name for a girl." She couldn't help herself in commenting on the young girl's name, but it seemed an obvious connection to the children's story. How odd she thought. "Umm yes, uh huh" said the girl. "You could say my parents had issues. They said it was supposed to be Jackie, but I guess the record keeper couldn't read my mother's writing or maybe misunderstood her when she spoke." Jack and Jill stood facing each other, each one thinking that there was a message in their meeting. Jill spoke first, "do you attend church?" she asked. Jack stared at the ground for a moment without responding, then, quietly said "no". "Well, that's ok" Jill responded. The pastor could feel the girl's apprehension and wanted to assure her that explanations were not necessary. "You're more than welcome to join us" Jill said. She went on and told Jack the day and time of the next service but knew in her heart that this little vagabond would not be attending. Not wanting to let her go she invited her to come the next day and join her for lunch. She was hoping to get to know her better, but also felt that the girl needed something in the way of friendship. Whatever it was, she was strongly attracted to the child-like demeanor that Jack possessed and knew in her heart that she should not be roaming the streets alone. She then asked her about the case Jack was carrying. "Oh" Jack replied, "this is my guitar. I play and write songs as they come into my head." Jill stared at the guitar case and saw that it was quite worn and wondered if the actual instrument looked the same. "Why don't you bring it with you tomorrow when you come? I'd love to hear you play." "I never go anywhere without it" Jack responded. Jack went on, "um, ok, I guess that would be fine." "On second thought I wondered if you had any place to stay tonight" Jill asked tentatively. The pastor did not want to scare the girl off. Jack explained that she was looking for a room. Jill offered to give her a lift to a modestly priced hotel at the end of town. Jack again looked at the ground, and speaking quietly said, "yes, thank you, that would be nice."

After dropping the little musician off Jill drove home in deep thought about how this waif had landed on her church stoop. She thought to herself that God certainly did have a sense of humor, and so the next day, as previously arranged, the pastor picked the girl up at her room and Jack and Jill arrived at the church together.

Chapter 2

The Woman Preacher

"I hope it isn't freezing in here", Jill spoke as she opened the front door of the church. Jack stood politely to the side. It was only 9am, a little early for her taste. Jill on the other hand seemed wide awake as if she had been up since dawn, which in fact she had. A light sleeper all her life, Jill found it difficult to lie around in bed once roused. "Ah" Jill sighed; it feels quite warm in here for a change. The transition from summer to fall could be an adventure in guessing, consequently the church thermostat got lots of action by well meaning staff, and members for that matter.

No one was around yet, so Jill took the opportunity to show Jack around the place. After going through the main sanctuary Jill steered Jack to the small kitchen so that she could put a little breakfast together before the day started. "We have some leftover sweet rolls and muffins here" Jill spoke. "I'll just heat them up in the microwave while the coffee brews." Jack was feeling shy about all the attention and consequently kept quiet. Her nod was enough, and Jill was very aware that the girl found it hard to speak to strangers. The meager breakfast was soon ready and the two sat down at a small table in the dimly lit room. Actually, the kitchen served the adjoining fellowship hall. The small table where they sat was primarily for anyone cooking; just a convenience and not in any way designed to warm a conversation. The utilitarian atmosphere wasn't helping Jill's cause in getting the girl to open up. Jack ate little but drank several cups of coffee and seemed satisfied. Jill wasn't one to push food on people but did notice that the girl hardly ate a crumb. "So" Jill asked, "how long have you been here?" "Just a few days" Jack responded. Jill wanted to inquire further but feared scaring the girl off so kept her silence. "I'd like to show you something" Jill said; waving her arm in the air she kindly commanded "come on."

Jill led the way down a long dimly lit hallway with Jack trailing behind. "This church building is over a hundred years old" Jill spoke. "You know I've never liked the phrase *going to church*" Jill went on. "It's just a building after all. You really don't need to be a Greek scholar to understand most of the things Jesus said. He referred to the human body as a temple; that's the building. But" ...; as Jill trailed off she took a sharp turn into a small room. Jack kept silent, rather liking to hear what Jill had to say. She got the feeling that this pastor was not the run-of-the-mill religious fanatic she was accustomed to. Jack wondered where they were going when Jill abruptly stopped. Jill had her hand on the corner of a bookshelf, and turning she looked at Jack with a most serious expression. "What I'm about to show you is sort of a secret" Jill spoke quietly. She went on. "If you'll just grab the corner there Jack, we can pull together." As they did, a small crack appeared, and as they pulled further on the shelf it became apparent that there was a door. This door had an unusual handle, kind of flat and looked like brass. Below the handle was a keyhole. Almost like something out of the Alice in Wonderland story. Jill reached into her pocket and drew out a key; a golden key. Jack thought it strange that something so old could be so bright; not tarnished at all. Jill found a light switch located on a wall to the left. She turned it on. It barely illuminated the staircase. It looked steep. Jack became a little fearful, wondering what Jill had in mind. Jill sensed the girl's apprehension and spoke softly; "don't be afraid. Just watch your step." The women descended the stairs together, and once at the bottom, Jill reached to the right and found another light switch. As she flipped it up several lamps came alive. There was no overhead lighting and the small room appeared quite cozy. Jill turned to look at Jack. The girl's expression had taken on an almost angelic hue. Jill was stunned but tried to appear casual. "So, what do you think?" the pastor asked. Jack's eyes roamed around the room taking everything in, as if drinking deeply of something mystical. She noticed the antique music stand first. Her eyes then focused on a small desk with a beautifully carved wooden chair. A brass lamp lit the top where papers might lay, a comfortable looking chair beside it. Up in the corner there appeared to be a small window that had been painted over. It was cracked slightly open and Jack could feel a warm breeze cross her face. "How unusual", she thought. It had been chilly before coming down to the basement room.

Jill was staring at the girl when Jack spoke first. "What is this?" she asked. "It's for you" Jill responded. The pastor went on; "several years ago while praying God gave me a vision of sorts. Please understand that I'm not given to such things, so it came as quite a surprise to me. The thought came as I was meditating that I needed to come down here and organize a room. At first, I thought it might be for meditation, but as time went on it seemed like I was compelled to furnish the place just as you see it. I thought it was interesting since I have absolutely no musical abilities at all. I saw the music stand at a junk store and had to have it. Some of the things were already here; like the desk. It looks like it's a million years old but never been used. I just sort of organized things and waited." "Waited?" Jack asked. "Yes" replied Jill. The pastor went on to explain that as she prayed each day, it seemed like the Lord was saying she had done her part and now He was going to finish the task. Jill looked into Jack's eyes and held out her hand. The girl looked down and the golden key glowed as if it was alive. "This is for you" the pastor said. Jack did not raise her hand immediately, but after a few moments she reached out and grasped the key; it felt warm from the pastor's touch. As Jack held it her heart skipped a beat. She could feel a rhythm inside and musical notes fairly danced in her mind."

"When can I come here?" Jack asked. "whenever you want. This is your place" Jill responded. The pastor went on to explain to the girl that as unusual as it seemed, it was important that she tell no one about the room. In fact, Jill was certain that the room had been vacant for many years, so she was not worried about anyone coming down. The only thing that seemed to connect the room to the church was a few wires for lighting. There were no maintenance machines to attend to. In fact, Jill was certain that in her many years as the church pastor, no one but herself, even knew about the place. The girl broke into the pastor's thoughts. "I'd like to bring my guitar down here now" Jack spoke. "Oh, yes, great" Jill responded. Before climbing the stairs to the sanctuary Jill told the girl she was welcome to use the room anytime and added that she would give her another key to open the side door of the church office. This would give her outside access. Since Jill had appointments arriving soon she began to climb the stairs. The women walked together and once at the top, the pastor knew that she had stepped out on a spiritual ledge, but really had no choice.

Chapter 3

Lilly and the Sidewalk

The sidewalk was alive with children; very unusual for a weekday in this part of town. It was still summer, however and even the bleak weather did not keep the scruffy rascals from wanting to play. The sun was setting, and the children spurred on by a chill in the air, began their scurry home. An old woman looked on from a corner street. Her arms were fairly full of purchases she had made earlier. Her heart knotted a bit looking at the small creatures. Things had happened that she no longer thought about, but the feelings were still there. The sun began to abruptly sink. A cold wind assaulted the old woman, and she grabbed her coat tightly around her frame, pulling a stocking cap down firmly. Suddenly it was dark. She looked from side to side contemplating crossing the street. She had seen the old church many times on her walks but avoided walking near it. As she looked up a bright light blinded her momentarily as a car rounded the corner. At precisely the same moment a lilting melody could be heard from somewhere. She thought to herself that maybe she was dying. And then, as if transported in time she heard the crass voice of a woman and the roaring of a car engine. She looked down and could see she was in a sleeping bag inside a small tent. "Get out! Get out of there!" the woman in the car shouted. Her gaping mouth opened again, "you're in my parking place"; venom fairly dripped from the open sepulcher. The old woman, now young, peeked out from the tent opening. "What?" she asked. "I said, get out of my parking place" the writhing image spoke again. Just then the girl Lilly, looked up and saw a sign. *Church Secretary* it said. The parking lot was empty, but it was apparent that this woman wanted her parking place. "I don't see your name anywhere" Lilly stated. The girl went on agitated; "so what's your name?" The woman in the car became even more livid, responding that if her parking spot was not vacated immediately she would call the police. "Vagrants are not allowed here" she continued. Elaborating, she said "this is not a campground and you can't do this. You cannot camp in a church parking lot. Don't you see that this is a church?" she fairly screamed. All the while the church secretary's foot was jammed on the accelerator spewing out fumes and hot air making the little tent quiver. "Ok, ok", Lilly shouted. The girl was scrambling to get her shorts on and told the woman so. "Just give me a minute" Lilly yelled. This had been a bad idea Lilly thought. "What the heck?", a man's voice filled the air. It was Lilly's boyfriend. He suddenly sat up asking again what the ruckus was about. "Oh, that old bitty in the car wants us out of here. I think she's crazy and might run us over," Lilly fumed. The young man, Carl, said it would be better to just get their stuff together and leave. This made Lilly irate, and even though she agreed, she was going to get the last word. As the couple scrambled to dress and get out of the tent the church secretary kept up a constant diatribe. While Carl dismantled the tent, Lilly walked to the side of the car with its engine still running and signaled for the woman to lower her window. She would not and spoke behind the glass. "You are breaking the law young woman and should be grateful that I don't call the police." This only fueled Lilly's anger. The girl thought to herself, "here I am in paradise, and now hell as arrived in the church parking lot." Just the day before she and Carl had called the local Christian shelter looking for a place to stay, and the man at the other end said he didn't have time to help them. He had gone on to say that after all, they had made it this far so surely, they could figure out what to do. Carl knew about church, but Lilly did not. And now, Lilly, and old woman stood on an obscure street wrapped in a musical cloak that came from far below. The sound was in her, speaking truth, exposing lies, like a shroud covering the wounds of the past. Abruptly Lilly was thrust into the past once again. All she could see was the sign *Church Secretary*. About the time that Carl had their things together a man drove into the church parking lot. He looked kindly and pulled into an unpaved portion of the lot. The sign in front of the hood of his car read *Clergy*. The man opened his car door and bounded across the parking lot to where Lilly and the church secretary were engaged. "What seems to be the matter?" he asked. Lilly, suddenly stood mute and Carl entered the picture with an outstretched hand.

The pastor shook it. Carl reiterated the previous day's folly in trying to find a safe place to camp. They were in Hawaii, and it appeared there were few such places. The incident with the previous day's phone call was recounted as well. At some point, the secretary roared into her spot and fled the scene. The pastor however showed some interest in the couple and in fact explained that the church was having a revival that very week and invited the two to come. There would be food, and this aroused Lilly's interest. It was decided that they would make their way back that evening and see what it was all about. Imagine Lilly's dismay upon walking across the parking lot seeing women wearing furs and fine dresses. All she had on was a tank top and an old army jacket over her shorts This image was burned into the old woman as the music played and she was transfixed on the street reliving the memory. Carl and Lilly made it as far as the church foyer. Men in suits were everywhere and one man did invite them into the sanctuary. When he opened the door, Lilly back pedaled to the nearest wall and fear akin to drowning engulfed her. She ran out as fast as she could, vowing never to go to another church as long as she lived. The music was intense now.

Down deep in the basement Jack's instrument resonated. She played notes that she had never arranged in quite the same way before. It was as if an unseen hand was guiding her fingers along the frets and she couldn't stop even if she wanted to.

Meanwhile, old Lilly was waking, as if from a dream. An intense light was burning her eyes as people spoke loudly. Wha? What? Lilly murmured to herself.

She was lying on the pavement unaware of the people around her. Her thoughts however were vivid. "Do you love me?" she asked God. "I wanted you to love me" she spoke to Him. "I'm here a voice said soothingly. "Are you God? Are you Him?" Lilly asked. Lilly went on. "I ran from the church but not from you. I broke the law. All these years I hid, hoping you would find me." "It's not like that the voice said. Continuing, the voice remained with Lilly and spoke kindness and affirmation; "You remembered me with the bread and the wine, and I knew you. I did find you" His voice spoke. The music became as intense as a vice, and then Lilly woke up.

The paramedics spoke among themselves making arrangements as to where to take the body.

Chapter 4

Edward and the Sidewalk

Jill arrived at the church early the next morning. She had no idea what happened the night before. She was anxious to see if Jack was in the basement and strode toward the hidden door. It was silent however, and she could see that the door was closed. Jack was not there. She would wait and see if the girl showed up later. Shortly a small rotund woman appeared. This was the church secretary, of sorts. Her name was Anna. She was a kindly woman and attentive to the pastors needs. It was an unusual alliance. Anna had been widowed for a number of years and she had never worked an actual job Her lot in life was to take care of her abrasive husband, until he died of course. She had been in a quandary about what to do with herself when Pastor Jill advertised in the church bulletin that she needed an assistant. It was a match made in heaven and Jill wondered many times how she managed without Anna's help.

"Good morning" Anna spoke first. "Oh, hello Anna" Jill responded. The pastor went on. "Would you like some coffee?" Anna declined the offer. She had been up since dawn and was ready for some activity, having emptied her own coffee pot at home. Her problem sleeping was no mystery to Jill. The two had talked at length about it and resolved that all of the advice out there just didn't work. It was a matter of learning to live with it. Abruptly there was a loud knock on the door. Anna rose to answer it. She was startled to see a policeman standing there. He asked to come in and Anna stood aside indicating he should just enter "Sorry to bother you" the officer said, "but I need to ask you a few questions about what happened here last night." Jill overheard the man and rose from her seat to greet him. "What are you talking about?" Jill asked. The officer went on to recount the circumstances of the deceased woman on the street. He asked if they knew her because there was no identification on the body. Jill was a little shocked and responded that there were vagrants who frequently passed by, but she hadn't had any interaction with anyone lately. After hearing the officer's recount of the event, the women were a little saddened by it. Both Jill and Anna felt they had a responsibility to reach out to anyone who came their way. It wasn't always easy, but they took God seriously in his mandate out of Matthew 25:35-36. Feeding the hungry, clothing the naked, etc. It was a commonly quoted scripture, however both agreed that it was easier said than done. After the policeman left, the two women discussed what he had said. There didn't seem to be anything they could do about it, so they continued on with their work.

Meanwhile, Jack slept in. She had become extremely tired after playing in the basement the previous night.

She had in fact, fallen asleep in the comfortable chair and woke up several hours after the event on the street. She knew nothing about the woman dying as she played. It was just as well, because such a thing would have disturbed her greatly. The girl mentally vowed to continue her playing as long as she could. It distressed her that for some unknown reason she was unable to write the notes that she played, so she memorized everything. There were always variations in her songs due to the inaccuracy of the method. It was uncanny though how she could duplicate a tune without writing down a note.

Chapter 5

Psalm 9

Edward walked the streets at night due to insomnia. He had remarkably strong legs due to this practice and could walk for miles at a time without tiring. This particular evening, he decided to take another route. As he rounded the corner of the rundown church the music caught his ear. He slowed his pace a bit and listened. It was transfixing. He had never heard anything like it. "What is it?" he thought to himself. He became mesmerized and totally unaware of his surroundings. Without realizing it he had lowered himself onto an old tree stump and using it as a chair he sat quietly. The melody carried him along and soon he was transported to a previous time.

The ship rolled violently while waiting along the coast of Korea. It was a conflict they said, however Edward, as a ships officer knew that they were in full battle mode. Suddenly a violent explosion erupted on the foredeck and Edward felt himself thrown against a bulkhead. Shrapnel sliced through parts of his back. He was one of the fortunate ones. Six seamen died that day, and it would be Edward's duty to notify family members. This event haunted Edward for the rest of his life. Night terrors would awaken him, and he never knew what would trigger these events. At times feelings of failure would haunt him and as the years went by he lost all hope of any future in the military. The explosion, as it turned out was an accident and not an assault on the ship. This further exacerbated his feelings of guilt toward the young men who died. What could he have done through observation of their errors to prevent such a tragedy?

Edward, a middle-aged man now, sat in the church pew listening. The pastor asked everyone to stand and greet their neighbor, something Edward did not mind doing. As he stood the tall lanky pastor headed his way. "Good morning!" the pastor declared reaching out his hand. Edward gripped the man's knuckles firmly stating his name. A couple sitting in front of him turned and offered their hands as well. It was all very lively Edward noted to himself. This particular denomination was usually sedate in their approach to worship, and the exchange surprised and pleased him. Things seemed to be looking up. After an ugly divorce, Edward wasn't anxious for any more confrontations. He was seeking God in his usual quiet way.

Edward attended the church for almost a year before even considering becoming a member. He threw himself into renovation projects, along with the couple that had befriended him earlier. Due to the small congregation there was little money to update things like the restrooms and children's meeting rooms. There were also a couple of tight fisted deacons who were opposed to spending money on much of anything. Actually, Edward and the couple paid for the construction supplies and did all the work themselves. Unknown to Edward this made him very unpopular with the folks in control. That is why the incident blindsided him. After the couple joined the church, Edward gave it a lot of thought, and at the prompting of the pastor decided to take the plunge and join the church as well.

It was arranged on the last Sunday of the month that he would meet with the deacons after the service. He was told it was a formality of this particular denomination. They basically asked the prospective member if they adhered to the doctrine of Jesus Christ as the Son of God. This is where the problem started. Of course, Edward believed all that, but was unaware that a particular deacon was not in favor of accepting him as a member. On the prearranged date, Edward arrived at church wearing his best suit. He was escorted to a back room after the service ended. The pastor told him to wait and the others would join him. The thought of this event overcame the man on the stump. He remembered it well. After waiting in the room for half an hour the pastor came in kind of flustered, stating that there was a mix up and asked if Edward would mind doing it another time. It seemed strange, but Edward said that would be fine. A few weeks later the same scenario was played out. Edward was told to wait in a room after the service, and of course had on his best suit. He replayed the event like it was happening again. After a long while the pastor entered the room, apologizing profusely and told Edward that there was a misunderstanding with one of the deacons. He was then told that he would be contacted soon about joining the church. Edward looked the pastor in the eye and asked him what was going on. "Well, it seems that one of the deacons refused to vote for you", the pastor responded. "Really" the pastor went on, "you should be thankful." "What?" Edward asked. The pastor responded; "these people aren't very nice and frankly, I'm hoping to get out of here soon myself" Edward couldn't believe his ears "You've got to be kidding" Edward said. And then he stood up, slowly shaking his head, turned his back to the pastor and exited the church. Edward's thoughts continued, and the beautiful music washed over him. He was remembering the pastor's wife visiting him shortly after the event. "I really feel like you're owed an explanation" she stated; "this is so embarrassing" she went on. "They did you a favor not voting you in. A couple of the deacons didn't like you and that's how they do things; believe me, I wouldn't go to that church myself if my husband wasn't the pastor." She concluded by saying that she was really sorry, and didn't want him to endure any more embarrassment, but there was no way he would be accepted by the church. Edward thought to himself that he wasn't the one who should be embarrassed. For years after the incident Edward rarely attended church. On his walk this evening, he was drawn to the music. Deeply resonating in the basement, the girl played flawlessly. The notes were driven into Edward, like individual spikes, opening wounds. He looked down and his hands were bleeding; blood was dripping from his side onto the pavement. "I've been shot" he thought." Another drive by shooting and now I'm the victim." His thoughts underscored by the sound from below. It was then that he realized the figure wasn't him at all. Reaching out with scarred hands was a man. "Here, let me help you up" the apparition spoke. "I didn't know that I was down"

Edward replied. "Do I know you?" Edward asked. "I know you" was the response; "but how?" Edward exhaled, and then took a deep breath and exhaled again, much as an exhausted swimmer might. Then all was still. Edward realized he was still sitting on the tree stump. The darkness was giving way to the dawn. The sun peeked through the fog as it appeared to whisper, and the faintest sound still came from somewhere. He stood and felt what could only be described as relief. For the first time in years his head was clear. As he looked at his surroundings he realized that he was alive, and beauty was everywhere. His heart fairly exploded with love and his only thought was that he had been given a reprieve. A heavy burden had been lifted and any thought of rejection had escaped through the imagined wounds. Edward began to walk and as he did, he noticed that the side door to the church was slightly ajar. As he approached it a wind caught it suddenly, slamming it shut. Just as he reached out to touch the handle a voice spoke. "This way Edward, I am the door'"

"BE KIND TO ME, GOD; I'VE BEEN KICKED AROUND LONG ENOUGH. ONCE YOU'VE PULLED ME BACK FROM THE GATES OF DEATH, I'LL WRITE THE BOOK ON HALLELUJAS; ON THE CORNER OF MAIN AND FIRST I'LL HOLD A STREET MEETING; I'LL BE THE SONG LEADER, WE'LL FILL THE AIR WITH SALVATION SONGS."

Psalm 9 – The Message, by Eugene Patterson

Chapter 6

Jack Dreams in the Basement

Jack arrived at the church just as the sun was setting. She had walked the entire day along the beach. Digging her toes in the sand was euphoric and she found that it was addictive. She just couldn't stop herself. Before she knew it, the time had run out and she wanted desperately to play, so she hurriedly made her way back to the church. Deep in her jeans pocket she could feel the key; the golden key, as Jill had called it. What an amazing thing it had turned out to be. At the same time, she felt the need to write out a dream she had the night before. It was amazingly real, and she hoped to recapture it. She soon found herself standing at the door of the church. The golden key fairly gleamed in the dark as she turned it in the lock. Once down the stairs she sat at the small desk, found a notebook and began to write.

As humans we superimpose our personal beliefs, assumptions, and prejudices over the truth of God's message; the sum of it being Love.

The world seeks to worship and declare that there is something greater than self. All of creation groans and aches for the coming of the Lord, for with that coming will be an end to suffering. Scales will fall from blind eyes and the truth will be revealed, exposing the centuries old lie that we are god and he is not. This fabrication is the outcrop of self-delusion. Somewhere at some time an unnatural creature bound the human race taking over the sound mind that God intended every one of his children to possess. A faltering unsure walk ensued creating generations of doubting people. A people who had been spiritually diluted and washed out; pale and without strength they continued in the lie, until at the end only a few remained.

A handful craved truth and in their search for it, cast off all worldly cares becoming nomads and strangers in the earth. Their lives seemed destitute, and yet they became full. Outwardly they took on the appearance of poverty, and yet God saw from heaven that they were rich. They became possessed by a holy sound and all who heard it stopped, transfixed, to listen. Hear what the spirit says to the churches. "Holy, holy, holy, is the Lord. The cries of the angel's trickle through the thick foggy layer of unbelief. "Holy is the Lord" they cry out, so that his ears can hear, and in the process this beautiful declaration filters down to the hurting people below. The greatest pain of all is the heart that has no assurance. The most deplorable condition is an empty human life. It is degradation beyond words, for the lie has raped and beaten the true spirit out of them, and they are in need of a savior. When the destitute reach out they are told that the savior has left, gone far, for who knows how long. Being told that he will return does not salve the hurt; they take matters into their own hands and begin to search, wandering to and fro throughout the earth. Letting go can only do this. If others are to join the search they too must lay down their earthly possessions. It is far too cumbersome to go on a hunt while carrying unnecessary burdens. They take only the essentials and the earth provides the rest. The earth and its fullness are the Lords. He will provide.

Critics abound when the resolute take a stand. The ears of the travelers must stay tuned to the spirit; for this is their guide and comforter. If a fellow traveler falls, then those closest must take respite from their own journey and carry the stricken one; feed them and nurture them until strength returns and they can resume their pilgrimage. Some travelers do not want to do this. They would rather build a hut for the fallen one and leave them behind. It would be a lot easier that way. Let a few of the slower travelers stay behind, while the strong ones go on "but the Lord said the race is not given to the swift and the strong but to him who endures." Ecclesiastes 9:11

Enduring what? Could it be someone else's weakness? Possibly, but the truth remains that all are weak, and it's just a matter of time before the weakness is exposed. It is in the bible that love covers all sins. Proverbs 10:12. The bible also says that all have sinned and fallen short of the glory of God, and yet, in my weakness, I am made strong.

So, the pilgrimage moves forward and reliance on

self is abhorred. Relying on one another is the key to success. Strong leadership is essential, and in wisdom the weakest and most profane are chosen to lead. Why is that? These are the ones humbled by failure and will readily seek wisdom from above; that is why. They know that only God knows the right path and so are less likely to lead others off the safe path into a ditch What happens on the spiritual trail is treated with reverence. To succeed no one is permitted personal luxuries at the expense of the others. One may bathe a filthy fellow traveler in a pure stream, washing them gently, and after patting them dry, apply soothing massage oil over the injured back and arms and legs that have been caught in briars along the way. The healing portion of the journey is another essential ingredient to keep the search for the truth alive.

At times, beds are made alongside the road and temporary camps sprout up. These are the encouraging tents. Souls are counseled one on one, in privacy, for some hurts can only be exposed in the safest conditions. Counselors are comprised of those with the most scars. These are the deeply healed ones. You know this because they have endured deep cuts, and even burns in obvious places on their bodies. Great respect is given when one encounters an encouraging tent. There is little talk anyway, but when a traveler comes upon one of these tents passing by becomes an act of worship, for the work done there has significant eternal implications.

Often the road of the traveler becomes treacherous. Steep inclines can make mountains seem impossible. For centuries there have been ones who have lived in hewn out rocks watching for those who struggle. They are the crippled ones. Their legs are bent at odd angles due to the many broken bones incurred while making their own climb. It is odd, but their twisted condition actually gives them a better grip and foothold while traversing over steep inclines. Many times travelers are tempted to go back because the way looks so hazardous, but save for the rock ones, they do go on. The crippled ones are highly regarded due to the skills they have developed. They are also quite humorous and seem to always be smiling. It is interesting to view their agility despite what appears to be a handicap. Here is where the pilgrim is invited to partake of a great dose of hope, the true antidote for despair. To say the least, this can be the most exhilarating part of any traveler's journey.

The voice in the dream was clear. Jack then heard the most beautiful music and looked toward a broken window and began to walk toward it. She desired above all things to enter in to the room where she could actually see the music dancing in the air as it played. It appeared there were people in there and just as she reached toward the broken glass a woman's voice spoke, gently, but firmly. "That is the healing room. You can't go in there yet." Jack abruptly woke up and could almost taste the beautiful sound and feel it flow through her body. "Was I dreaming?" she questioned herself, and then rose from the chair to play.

Chapter 7

Lindsey on the Sidewalk
(John Chapter 9, an Allegory)

Fog rolled in as the sun set its flame. The small city took on the hue of amber while the young woman sat alone in the basement of the church. The silence was deafening. How many times would she be on the brink of misunderstanding God? Or would she forever live in fear and distrust? The stringed instrument seemed to lay in repose. She gently brushed her fingers along the frets and soon a new song emerged.

A dark-haired woman appeared at the corner of the church. She suddenly looked up and appeared disoriented. She had been deep in thought and taking long strides in an attempt to alleviate the anger and hurt she had been feeling. Out of nowhere a melody floated above her and in her. It was music, but also some kind of message she could not quite discern. In the blink of an eye she was transported to another place and time.

Lindsey walked with a purpose and command

belying her rather small frame. She was cutely boyish with short black hair that stood straight up. The look was intentional. She chose her style with purpose. During her youth she was forced into a mold that frankly suffocated her. She knew she was different at an early age. She detested the *girl stuff* forced on her. It was confusing, to be quite honest. Julie looked at her friend and spoke candidly. "This can't go on" she said. "What do you mean?" Lindsey countered. Her voice rising slightly, she went on. "I don't understand what you want." Julie sat in silence for a few minutes before speaking. "We're Christians and can't have these kinds of feelings for each other. It will send us both to hell. At least that's what the church says." Lindsey shot back heatedly; "oh right, you believe some antiquated belief that some old fools wrote in the bible. The same bible that says owning slaves and women was alright." She didn't want to go on, but in her mind, she was recounting dozens of church customs and beliefs that had changed according to the customs of the day. Feeling a loss of control, she bit her lip and looked away. Her mind was reeling. She looked down and it appeared the fog had settled all around her legs and she couldn't even see her feet. Then her body felt enveloped in warmth and she could feel someone's arms actually wrap completely around her and the heat intensified like a warm bath. A voice spoke softly as she rocked back and forth. "My little dear one" it said. Fearful to answer Lindsey allowed her body to collapse into the welcoming arms. Lightness overcame any resistance to flee and she felt herself eager to hear the voice again. Then panic arose as she realized that she could not see.

"I'm blind! Oh God, I'm blind" she shouted. "Julie, Julie are you there?" No answer came. Only the distant sound of music resonated in her ears. The arms continued to hold on, even as Lindsey tried to break free. "Who are you?" she demanded. No answer came. Lindsey then had the sensation that she was sitting on a soft pillow as she leaned back against the one holding her. The arms were strong and yet tender. Not wanting to leave and yet curious to see who had such a hold on her she turned to look but the arms held her firm. A voice spoke; "I'm not letting you go. No matter how long you ignore me I'm here forever. Whenever you run, you cannot out run me. No matter where you hide, I will find you. You have always been my dear little one. The only abandonment you will feel from now on will be total abandonment in me." Lindsey looked down and saw a child's feet. They were her feet. She felt confused, and at the same time, knew that she was experiencing something profound. This was strange and yet so normal. When she tried to look at her surroundings all she saw was darkness, and yet she could see the little feet. They had no shoes on and were quite dirty. It looked like they had run through every dirt heap in existence. Lindsey was recalling her childhood while she gazed at the bare feet. How she would run everywhere she went. Her mother would constantly yell at her to slow down, and say things like, "why do you run everywhere Lindsey? Why can't you just slow down and walk?" It seemed she was always in a hurry and in the process took quite a few falls. She remembered once running and climbing over a fence and jumping down on the other side, only to drive a nail straight up into her right foot It took another child to pull the nail out and blood squirted everywhere. She ran home screaming the entire way. Then she remembered her mother after seeing all the blood, with panic in her voice picked her up bodily and carried her to the bathtub and ran cold water over her foot. It seemed to bleed forever, and as the blood washed down the drain, Lindsey remembered her mother carrying on about it, and yet through the throbbing wound, she was glad that her mother had hugged her and would have jumped on another nail for the loving concern she showed. Lindsey began to sob. She could not stop. It went on and on. The arms continued to hold tightly. "Why?" she asked when she could finally speak. "Why what?" the voice responded. "Why was I born like this?" "How is that Lindsey?" "You know", Lindsey went on. "No, I don't know" the voice said. "I can't explain it" Lindsey said. "But you're a little chatter box Lindsey, and yet you can't just come out with what's really bothering you." The voice went on. "I've heard your heart's cry many times over the years my dear little one. You know the truth, but until you acknowledge it you will not be set free." "You're mean" Lindsey replied. "You know that I'm not mean little one, so why do you say that?" "Because you want me to say something that I just can't put into words." The voice went on, "no, you can put it into words, you just don't want to." Lindsey remembered going to a psychologist a few years before and it was completely futile. For almost a year, she met with a counselor and told him absolutely nothing about herself, or how she really felt inside. There were a few times when she came close to revealing her soul, but then she would catch herself and withdraw. It was a matter of trust.

Lindsey felt like she had fallen into what could only be described as timeless surrender. The world had ceased to exist. The voice had grown silent, and yet the arms still remained. She was thinking about what a friend had said about Christianity. It boiled down to the idea that people talk a lot about their point of view regarding Jesus, but few people actually *do* what Jesus said to do. Confrontations emerge about salvation because people want to believe that there is inherent goodness in most of humanity, therefore being accepted by God is contingent on doing good things. The whole *God in the flesh* thing unhinges all of that. Why bother to disconnect from heaven, and come to earth, and be nailed to a cross? Isn't that the gospel story? A substitutionary sacrifice completed the process. Oh, and let's not forget the resurrection. There must be a pretty deep wound of sin to overcome, or frankly, it doesn't make a bit of sense. Lindsey's thoughts were interrupted by the voice. "I'm hearing you now Lindsey", he spoke. He went on, "imagine yourself the man born blind. You are trying to explain your healing. "What would you say?" he asked. Lindsey thought for a minute before answering. "I don't know" she said. She thought within herself and a story began to emerge. She heard a question. "Who sinned? This girl or her parents, causing her to be born blind." Suddenly, she was standing in the midst of a small crowd and was being questioned about her healing. They were looking at her intently, demanding to know the answer to their question. She answered by first telling them they were ridiculous. She went on. "You want to blame someone for whatever you perceive to be wrong. When things don't appear perfect, and in fact are imperfect according to your standards you have to lay blame. How could I sin while in my mother's womb? I wasn't even born yet and you're asking if I sinned. What opportunity did I have to do anything other than grow big enough to be born? Explain to me why I would be punished for something my parents did wrong. You're looking for cause and effect. God is bigger than your accusations. Look at me you say, because you want everyone to think that you're good, and you aren't."

Lindsey thought to herself that she should just be quiet but once she started she couldn't stop. "My feelings were always different, even as a child. You wouldn't understand. I lived my whole life under an umbrella of shame and condemnation. It boils down to the fact that I was born blind and crippled. Not physically, but spiritually. Then I was raised in a dark place much of the time. When the light would occasionally break through, my spirit would start to rejoice, but the spiritually dark world where I lived would do everything in its power to block out the light. I certainly did not personally know where the light came from, but I made many futile attempts at chasing it down. But the harder I ran the more elusive the light would become. Lots of times I just gave up trying to grab it. I would watch it fade into the distance, much like a sunset. As the light would go out, and darkness would emerge, just like the sunset, there would be a slight afterglow, so it never became completely dark. It sounds as if Jesus was running away from me, making me pursue Him, only to let me down by getting too far ahead of me. No, that's not what was happening. Jesus was wooing my distant heart. I was like the man born blind. People questioned me and condemned me, mostly behind my back, but Jesus continued to explain my situation with love, not condemnation. Like the man born blind, my relatives and those who knew me would talk among themselves. They would say I was a sinful girl who was spawned by sinful parents, or maybe I was just born like that, sinning my way out of the womb. Others would say, no, she's someone else. It just looks like her. But then when questioned I would say yes, it's me. They would want to know why I was walking around with my head held up, acting like I was the most loved person in the world, while everyone knew the truth of my dark life. "Who did this to you?" they would demand to know. They would question me over and over wanting to know how it happened that I became loved with such intensity. I would tell them, "He spit on me. Jesus was in town, but of course I didn't know who he was because I was born spiritually blind. One day I was begging on the corner like I always did, and he walked right up to me and Jesus rubbed something that felt like mud on me. When I turned to look at him I fell over kind of in a vision, and I was being hurled into a river and then felt myself being lifted out of the dark water and that's when I saw it." You saw what?" they demanded to know. "The light" I said. A huge enveloping light wrapped me up and it felt really warm and soothing. Then I saw his smiling face and heard him say "I was sent," Jesus said he was sent to earth to get me. Then he said, "I'm washing you clean. All of the stains from the rotten things thrown at you are gone." He said a lot of other things about what he would be doing for me in the future. I asked him if he knew what I had done, and he said "yes, Lindsey, I was with you the time you felt so hopeless that you tried to end your life. You kept trying to stop breathing but I held you in my arms and breathed for you until help came. You almost left earth too early, but I had much for you to do. My love breathed new life into you and then you were able to breathe on your own. But you needed help, and I tried hard to recruit some of my friends to help you. For the most part they didn't listen but then I sent my special friend who took up residence inside of you."

Over and over I've been questioned about my new sight. When I try to explain and answer the questions I feel like I'm on a witness stand being tried for treason, or even murder. Everywhere I go the same people demand to know how I dare to talk about how much love Jesus showed me. Then one day it occurred to me that maybe they wanted to become his disciples too, so I asked them if that was why they were always questioning me. They got really mad at me and threw me out into the street. I was only trying to answer their questions about the goodness of God. When they demanded to know where Jesus was, I told them he as in my heart and that's when they became livid and called me a piece of trash and said that I wasn't deserving of the real god like they had. I can still hear them in my head sometimes. The voices say, "you're less than a piece of dirt. Don't try and come into our house, or worse, the house of God." Over and over I can feel the grip of their hatred and so many accusations that I'll never be any good, and they're probably right.

But I don't mind it when they say I'm a disciple of that man, not a disciple of their god.

I found it amazing that they claimed not to know anything about Jesus, but there I was, a testimony to his goodness. When I told them, Jesus was from God it really made them mad. That's when they said I was nothing but dirt. I guess Jesus didn't follow all the religious rules when he helped me, since it was one of their holy days or something when he spit in the dirt and put the mud on me.

A funny thing happened after getting thrown out of pretty much everything, and into the street. Someone told me that when Jesus heard about it he came looking for me. I was feeling really low and depressed, not to mention humiliated, so I went back to my corner where I previously begged and sat on the ground. I saw his feet first, and then he leaned down and put both of his hands on my face and pulled my head up until I was looking right into his eyes. "Do you believe I am the Son of God?" he asked. "show me where he is mister, so I can believe in him" I answered. "You're looking right at him "Jesus said. He went on. "I know you recognize my voice." And I did.

Suddenly there was light all around Lindsey but the arms holding her were gone. Julie looked down with concern and asked what happened. "I've been looking for you all night" she said. They were both quite old now. Lindsey reached her hand toward her friend and Julie took hold pulling her up. "I love you", they both said it at the same time, and continued their walk down the street arm in arm.

Chapter 8

Jill Reflects

Jill stood at the window overlooking the great river. What a fabulous view she thought. It was nice to have the luxury of a faraway viewpoint of life. Most of what she dealt with involved problems, and controversy, and pain; so much pain. However, Jill was an optimist by nature, so the calling of minister suited her. What occupied her mind lately was the little musician Jack. She rarely saw her since handing over the keys to the basement. It was obvious the girl had been there many times over the past several months. When she went to the basement it seemed much warmer now. Jill surmised that human touch had a powerful influence over the environment. She felt that way for a long time. Unfortunately, the congregation she led held to old fashioned beliefs, and even the mention of other-worldly things could cause a stir. She had attempted introducing healing services with soothing music and meditation, but with much resistance. It seemed the older crowd in the congregation was against it. They preferred the old hymns, with lots of piano banging. Thankfully the Lord had provided a worship leader more in tune with the current form of music, and praise songs were introduced at every opportunity. Jill would sometimes find herself almost dancing down the aisle as the music played and the candles were lit while she made her way to the front of the church. Her personal view of Jesus was that he was a happy man. We should be the same she thought. It was time to start working on next Sunday's sermon, so Jill turned toward her small den. The neat little desk suited her, and she would meditate before beginning to write. Jill prayed for the Lord to open her mind and spirit so that she could prepare a message from him. Sometimes random thoughts would come to her and she would dig into the bible praying for inspiration. A thought crossed her mind; we are so small. It went from there.

Chapter 9

Lucy and Sophia on the Sidewalk

Did you know that I loved you my friend? Not a carnal kind of love, but a love of respect for who you are. You were Sophia Loren, and I was Lucille Ball. Somehow, we were dropped off at the same place and time, without friends, and repelled by the locals.

The music played eerily as the woman walked down the street. Fog lined the trees. The mist flowed under the leaves as the dampness wilted her hair. She looked up, and saw her friend standing beside her on the sidewalk. It was morning, and they were waiting for the bus to take them to the awful High School where no one wanted to be their friend. Smoke erupted from Lucy's lips as she puffed hard on the Marlboro cigarette, hoping to finish it before their ride came. She looked toward Sophie with a twinkle in her eye. They both had the same thought. Maybe if they lingered when the bus arrived the driver would just leave, and they could go home for the day. Neither girl wanted to face the tormentors who lined the halls of the huge school. Lucy thought to herself that she might be dreaming. The song played on and the longer she stood the deeper she fell into the past. The street was now the street that the girls lived on. They both came from large families; Sophie's having two more children than her own. There was abundant love in one, and anger and bitterness in the other. Sophie's parents had a great love affair, and Lucy's introduction to love was demanding and angry. Sophie's dad had long ago conquered the demon of alcohol, and for years led others out of the deep waters of addiction. Lucy's parents were self-indulgent and hard-core drinkers while trying to feign the appearance of a normal family life. Smoke wafted the walls in both homes, but that is where the similarity ended. Any escape would do for Lucy. She loved to laugh and make others laugh too. Lucy remembered so many things as she stood along the road. It was comforting to have her friend again. It was such an easy friendship, with music, drinking coffee and playing cards at Sophie's kitchen table; smoking cigarettes, long before anyone knew of their harmful effects on the human body.

The bus pulled up and Lucy grabbed her friend's arm dramatically, saying "just one more puff!" The driver held the door open for a few more seconds after the others boarded. He then flung a disgusted look their way slamming the door shut, yelling that he was not waiting for them anymore. He drove off in a great cloud of diesel smoke and the girls laughed all the way back to Sophie's house. Sophie's mother was dismayed that they had missed the bus, as they told her a small lie. "Well I guess you two can just stay in your room and read", she said. That suited the girl's fine and they spent the rest of the afternoon looking at movie magazines and reading True Story magazines.

Lucy felt a cold chill run through her heart as she looked at her sick friend in the hospital. No one knew what was wrong with Sophie, but when she was discharged home, she never returned to school again. It was so sad, for Lucy had lost her cohort, even though they remained friends. In due time Lucy obtained her driver's license but Sophie did not. Then Lucy's parents decided to move again several miles away and there were very few times spent at Sophie's house. It was an unfortunate turn of events for Lucy. She drew strength from just being in Sophie's home. While they remained friends, it just wasn't the same, and Lucy began to experience what would later be diagnosed as clinical depression; a condition that would haunt her for most of her adult life.

Lucy's thoughts came in a rush. She thought to herself, "I lost my best friend."

Now, sitting at her computer, she looked at her Facebook page and saw her friend's name. What?, what is this? Someone with her friend's name was making an inquiry. "Are you the same Lucy who hung around with me in High School?" An onslaught of memories bombarded Lucy's mind. She was riding on a train to Los Angeles with Sophie. Lucy's parents had split up and her mother had become a sometimes-violent drunken woman. She had run after Lucy with a hammer, so she had locked the bedroom door and climbed out the window. After calling Sophie from a phone booth, she was taken to her friend's house to stay. They both decided to embark on an adventure to visit

Sophie's cousins in Southern California. The train ride was a grueling 14 hours, and it really took the fun out of riding the rails again for a very long time. They arrived disheveled but intact. Sophie spoke, "I can't stay here." "Why?" Lucy asked. "I just want to go home" Sophie answered. "I can't go home" Lucky stated. Lucy thought to herself; "this sucks. I don't have a home to go to." She ended up looking up an old friend of her mother's and the woman took her in. From that time on, Lucy just kind of wandered from one situation to another. Now, here she was, standing alone on a street in another forsaken town. But then, she remembered her friend. She answered the inquiry, and excitedly gave her phone number. During their conversations Sophie remarked that her husband said that whenever she mentioned *my friend,* he knew that she was talking about Lucy. He even commented to her one day; "do you realize that the only person you say *my friend* about is Lucy?" Of course, Sophie had many friends and people loved her dearly, but there was a bond in the friendship that even the years between had not obscured. Lucy was moved when Sophie shared this information with her. Sophie could not have known the despair that Lucy had experienced upon the death of her husband two years earlier. Her thoughts had continually assailed her that she would be alone forever. In fact, she had begun to believe that her unimportance and connection to anyone had propelled her into an abyss. Only her knowledge of God had kept her. He spoke to her heart daily. "I will never leave you or forsake you." Sophie's introduction back into her life had acted as a catalyst, brightening her days, and given her hope for

Lj Orten

the future. Seeing God like that, in someone else relieves the stress of looking for hope. Hope just dropped down from heaven in the form of her friend.

The music continued to play.

42

Chapter 10

David on the Sidewalk

David had spent many years playing guitar in a band in bars and night clubs, and now he couldn't quite remember why he was even walking down this particular street. If you had any doubts about this man's past, he quickly dispelled any idea's that he was in line for sainthood. His thoughts were as direct as his speech, and in his quiet delivery he made you feel like he was right there with you. Not like so many people that you talk to or attempt conversation with. In today's world people are so distracted and it can be unnerving at times. David felt a wave of guilt wash over him as he heard a distant sound. He stopped and stood as still as a deer anticipating a wolf or other predator. He had no fear, just anticipation. His thoughts turned to his past, something he tried to avoid. The music intensified and soon he was caught up in a distant memory.

The woman pulled in beside his RV and after some hesitation sort of fell out of her vehicle. She lived in the trailer next to his overlooking the river. "Hi", he spoke, and she turned and smiled a crooked grin at him. He was sitting outside playing his guitar when she pulled in. They had a short conversation about the grueling heat and humidity when David said, "I hear you play guitar." The woman shook her head and replied, "gee, I wonder who told you that." She knew very well who and commented about the impish young girl who lived in the park as well. She went on, "I don't actually play the guitar as much as it plays me. I play *at* it you might say." He responded by suggesting that they get together some time and *jam*. "I really don't play that well" she replied, "but ok that sounds fine." A couple of weeks went by and one evening they did get together and found a common meeting ground, musically speaking, and shared some songs that they both knew. It was obvious from the start that David was a skilled musician, but it didn't seem to intimidate the woman.

Jack's playing had by now infused the air and David found himself sitting on the ground with his back leaning against a light pole. His thoughts had taken him far away and he was being transported to a different time and place.

"I have an addictive personality" David said, as he took another pull on his cigarette. "I really don't deserve the good things that God has done for me. I was into drugs in a big way, for a long time with a lot of people. My upbringing had nothing to do with it. It was just something I wanted to do, and once I started it was almost impossible to quit." David was remembering his conversations with the woman, and over a period of a year they covered a lot of ground and he managed to piss her off a few times. He felt like if he spoke *his* truth that it should make people mad at some point or it really wasn't truth at all. The woman certainly wasn't shy about expressing her viewpoints either, and amazingly they never actually came to blows. David had a way of staying level so to speak, and not let his anger show, because after all, he was considering this woman to be a friend. It was obvious that their spiritual journeys had intersected in a run-down muddy river campground that in no way represented a resort atmosphere. They had commented to each other about the shabbiness of the place many times. Basically, it was their jobs that had brought them there, as well as the other campers. Everyone worked, and it was a place to land at the end of the day, and that was about it.

"I have something to want to talk to you about" David said, just as the woman was heading for her trailer. David was remembering the conversation. They had settled into the two camp chairs beside the woman's trailer drinking ice-cold beer to ward off the suffocating heat and humidity. That was their reasoning anyway. "You probably won't like this" David began, "but I left the last church I was in because of a doctrinal disagreement with the pastor. Actually, the pastor asked me to leave because I wouldn't agree with him and that was fine with me, but it hurt. The woman looked directly at him trying to anticipate what possible difference the two men could have had. David went on, "I believe that a person *can* lose their salvation. I don't believe that it's a once and for all deal with Jesus, and you have to live your faith and if you fail to do that then your salvation is in jeopardy." The woman began shaking her head as in *no way do I believe that*. The ensuing conversations regarding this issue became a point of contention at times and the two avoided talking about it much. The issue of *eternal security* prompted many discussions regarding spiritual matters and in fact, as David looked back he could see that there was a framework of God in just about everything they talked about. The woman was a liberal in every sense of the word, and yet still as passionate about the Lordship of Jesus as any human could be. Sandwiched in with all of the God talk, was beer drinking, guitar playing and singing; not always in that order. Through it all a friendship was emerging, and David commented that between the cussing and praising this was one crazy lady. Just the kind of person he could relate to. They provoked each other in a good way, and David felt like more friendships should be forged in the fire of disagreement. The woman felt the same way. She also believed that there were many paths that could lead to God, but He (God) was still the God of the bible when all was said and done. She too had been asked to leave more than one church because her views were not always in agreement with the status quo according to the Americanized version of Jesus teachings. "It's all about forgiveness" she would frequently say, and then get pretty mad about things, not at all concerned about the obvious contradiction.

The music played drawing David into its sound. It once took drugs to allow David the luxury of complete abandonment, but this was something other-worldly, and for once he had no desire to play along. It occurred to him that being in control had become a huge part of his DNA. His mind was being transformed, and it was through no effort on his part. How does that happen? David questioned the thought. Men live lies, and then must justify their actions creating a web of deceit that is so pervasive that only an outside source can bring deliverance. David was thinking about the woman's comment regarding the southern gospel she had grown to detest. "I wasn't always a Christian", she spoke with the matter of fact way she had. She went on, "I really believe a person has a time to believe, and it has very little to do with personal will. When you think about it, believing in God comes naturally to a child, but once adulthood sets in it becomes increasingly difficult to surrender that will and contemplate the after-life, which in reality, spiritually speaking, is a new way- of life in the flesh. She suggested that they go and visit some of her friends. David was all for it. During their conversations the woman had mentioned a couple who lived next door to her, and it was obvious that she held them in high regard. In particular she would talk about the man who just happened to be a minister, as well as a logging truck driver. "You really need to meet Pastor" she said. "There's something unbelievably sweet about him." She wasn't one to throw around compliments, so it fired up his curiosity. From the moment they entered the couple's house it was obvious that the Holy Spirit lived in the place

The music continued to play softly in the back of David's mind. It seemed to be everywhere, even coming from deep within his own spirit. His thoughts were becoming awkward and he was having a hard time keeping himself from mentally rambling. "I've seen the devil", David spoke to the woman. She gave a blank stare and then responded with a question, "where?" "It was in a church" David said. "So", the woman left the word hanging obviously waiting to hear the details. David went on. "He was the Pastor of the church I attended at the time. It was rumored that he thought of himself as the great comforter to certain women in the congregation had many sexual conquests. I didn't like him because I knew it was true and after the service one Sunday the preacher reached out his hand to me and I literally jumped back and yelled, *don't touch me you devil!* I could feel the evil in him and saw Satan in his eyes. I never went back and later found out that he was eventually asked to leave."

David had been relating the story while driving to the woman's friend. He went on to say that since that incident he rarely attended church services. What David did not know was that his expectations for spiritual renewal would not be disappointing.

Jack played throughout the night with little pause. There was a driving force in her that propelled her on. The man on the street, David, was lying on his back. It appeared he had fallen asleep, or perhaps died. No one was there to see what had taken place, and it would be morning before he was found.

"I am in control", the thought crossed David's mind. He knew that he was always in control. His mantra had been, and always would be that he would never be controlled by anyone or anything. And yet, his body was immobile and while his mind was alert, he was unable to move even a finger. His thoughts turned to his guitar; the one instrument in his life that was reality and escape, all at the same time. A fleeting thought crossed his mind, and it was simply this; that as far as he was concerned, he could do what he wanted, when he wanted, and yet was still unable to move. The sound permeating the air wafted his senses and while he considered the intricacies of what he was hearing, his heart seemed to melt within his chest. It wasn't altogether unpleasant, and David was tempted to allow the temptress sound to wrap him up, but somehow, he could not submit, and a great struggle ensued.

"I've written a verse for you", the voice spoke; "and it goes like this, rock of ages broken for you I gave my life to make you new. Rock of ages smashed and crushed, crossed a boundary to a land so lush." The voice continued, "rock of ages I stand alone…." But before it continued David screamed a scream to curdle the blood, "stop! Just stop!" An anger and despicable anguish rose up within the man lying on the ground, and yet the voice continued. "Rock of ages, before you were born carved a sacred place, filled with scorn." And one string at a time pulled the sound from Jack's instrument, at once gentle and even profane. The voice continued its refrain, "rock of ages, I stood your ground, and ground you down, pleasing me to give you sound…." And a gasp, as of a last breath emerged from the man David and he shuddered and shook like one taken from a cold, cold tomb, sounding like nothing more than a guttural release and deep moan, he softly said "let me go." And yet the voice was unrelenting, saying, "rock of ages, hewn for you, carved from stone and squeezed like dew, dripping love to bring you through…" And David lifted his head, if only in his mind to look and see where the sound came from but was blinded by it and it engulfed his body, and he gasped for air, but none came and with a resounding exhale became as quiet as the light that descended.

A local beggar found David's lifeless body lying on the pavement. It was pre-dawn and under cover of semi-darkness he rifled through the pockets of the lifeless man. The were all empty save for one strange looking piece of plastic; an almost transparent looking guitar pick. The beggar handled it for a moment, and in an instant placed it back into the man's pocket. His thoughts were as transparent as the small tool that was used to bring vibrant sound to a silent instrument. It wasn't worth stealing, for it had no worth without the hand to transform it.

Chapter 11

Jesus Left the Building

There was a joke that went around for years and became a commonly used term after the singer Elvis Presley died. I think it was because his fans really hated the thought that he was no longer alive they would fabricate sightings of him. Then people would mockingly say, "Elvis has left the building" which simply meant there was no way you were going to see him.

In today's culture in America there seems to be a church on every corner, but I declare to you, "Jesus has left the building." In fact, if I understand the scriptures correctly, the follower of Christ *is* the building." So, what has happened? Since I'm not God the following is an opinion, not sacred script, but there are a few things that seem to stand out.

My personal reading of the Bible leads me to believe that the central point of Christianity is not what we have done but rather what Jesus has done for us. I base this on several key scriptures; John 3:16, John 1:17, and Romans 6:23. There are obviously a lot more scriptures but for the sake of argument, it was obvious that Jesus declared He was the only way to God the Father. There's a lot to take in here, but the point I'm trying to make is that the foundation of the building (we being the building) is Jesus. Everything else hinges on the foundation. So, once I accept, internalize and believe that my sins are forgiven because of the accomplishment of Jesus on the cross, I become aware that I am brand new, reborn, born from above, and am now the property of God in all portions of my life and my eternity is sealed. The awareness factors in due to grace of God. I believe the veil is lifted giving the believer a viewpoint of truth that always existed in that person's life. There are many scriptures that describe such a thing; for instance, the Apostle Paul, formerly called Saul was a very religious man, and was in fact a Jewish Pharisee. He was literally blinded on the Damascus road and then his sight was returned, and he was filled with the Holy Spirit. In the book of Acts chapter 9:18 describes "something like scales fell from Saul's eyes and he regained his sight." (Amplified Bible) Many people ask if God is directing our lives, even in our unaware state. That is for every individual to decide. What happens after conversion is in God's hands, and the scripture is clear that human beings cannot earn their salvation or make it any more effective by personal life experience. Romans 3:23-25 makes it abundantly clear that we are brought into God's kingdom by grace.

Those buildings called churches are brick and mortar places where the church, the body of Christ meets. Or, at least that's what is supposed to happen. But is that what really takes place?

What many of us hear are arguments over doctrine, which is like debating over window dressing in an operating room while a patient is dying. Let me tell you something, operating rooms are scary places to be if you aren't trained in medicine. The lights are really bright, and for the safety of everyone concerned all possible steps are taken to maintain a sterile environment in an effort to prevent infection while a wound is open. Hello! Jesus healed the sick the diseased, and the outcasts of his day. He is the great physician so believe me when I tell you; He is the only one capable of knowing where to cut so the wounded are made whole. Who do we think we are, telling people that they can lose their salvation? How would you like it if a surgeon, right in the middle of your operation, decided that in her opinion, you were not worth the effort because it was just too hard to get to the tumor that was cutting off your air supply? Part of the Hippocratic oath reads; "I will prescribe regimens for the good of my patients according to my ability and my judgement and never do harm to anyone. It sounds like good advice to all followers of Christ.

Chapter 12

The Bride and Jesus on the Sidewalk

You make me cry! My silent scream is a gentle outpouring of rain sent to soothe your weary soul. You cannot hear me. You cannot see me. My music is a written sound that is transcribed wordlessly.

You judge me from the comfort of your windowless soul, affirmed in your hate, and you use my name to do it. I am weeping from the heavens and the rain pours down in torrents, for you are lost but not alone. The one who sits beside the still waters has run away from you. You have driven out the peace and replaced it with a performance. You make demands from the destitute. In your attempt to wash yourselves clean you use water gained from the sewer, filled with refuse and the sad, sad thing is it has become perfume for you, and now you don't even know the difference because your sense of smell has departed. The fragrant offering that I desire is not reflective self-worth; it is denial of self. Your appetite for hate has consumed you and you live in a palace of graven images that can never comfort the bereaved, the broken, the lost, the scared, the hungry, the diseased, the lonely, the beaten, the used, the forgotten, the betrayed, the sin sick soul, the naked, the wounded, the branded, the misunderstood, the promise breaker, the souls that cry out, Why?!!

The music drifted across the road, almost more of a feeling than a sound. The young girl leaned against the light pole, however it was quite dark because the bulb had burned out long ago and no one cared enough to replace it. The darkness was comforting to her. It was better that no one see what she really looked like. Ugly scars marred her once beautiful face. She had tried everything to cosmetically cover up the wounds and nothing worked. She looked at her dress, once beautiful, and now dirty and torn. Her beautiful wedding garment destroyed. Then a beautiful sound became clear and she looked up to see a bronzed hand reaching out to her. The closer she got to the apparition, the warmer she felt. It was cold outside. The voice spoke softly, "here, come here my pride and my joy. Let me wash you in the pool of my love. The rules have almost ruined your beauty, but I am much more powerful than you give me credit for." An unexplained fear gripped the girl. "I can't come any closer or I'll die"; she thought it, and while the words never departed her lips her visitor heard it. "Yes, you will, but that is only so that you may live. Do not fear. I will stay with you for this is the way of truth, and then you will be free. Understand me; I am able to catch you if you fall. My strength will become your strength, my forgiveness will become your forgiveness, and my acceptance will become your acceptance. You are not alone.

Chapter 13

The Conversation

Jack had walked the rocky beach for most of the night. Her mind would fill and then empty out. She knew she had one more song to play and waited for the silent queue which came from deep within her spirit. She made her way back to the church in the early morning hours. As she approached the steps that would take her down to her private sanctuary Jill came from behind. "Hello!" Jill exclaimed. "How are you little one? I haven't seen you in a while." Jack turned to face her friend. "Oh, I've been busy "Jack replied. "Well" Jill responded, "I have something to tell you and I hope it doesn't upset you. I've been offered a pastorate back East and have decided to take it. The real truth is, I've reached retirement age but don't feel like it's time for that yet. My family has been after me to move closer and I'm taking this opportunity to kind of kill two birds with one stone. How are you doing Jack?" Jill questioned the girl. "I'm fine" Jack responded and went on. "I too feel like my time here is coming to a close, so I guess the timing is perfect. I have one more project to complete and will be on my way. I hope to be finished in a day or two. Will the room still be available to me?", she questioned Jill. "Oh of course it is. I still have a lot of loose ends to attend to and won't be leaving for at least another month." At that Jack explained that she was going down to her sanctuary and they parted ways. Jill looked intently at the little waif and felt tenderness and sorrow at her leaving. She wanted to ask questions but had learned not to inquire too much into her new friends plans. There were times when Jill would be leaving the church and she would hear the ethereal sound coming from beneath the stone steps. Several times she would take pause and stand to listen, but then a strange thing would happen, and she would feel like she was eavesdropping on a private conversation prompting her to take flight. As she returned to the task at hand, it occurred to Jill that there had been an unusual amount of activity during the night hours on the corner across the street from the church. She had personally experienced a new feeling of peace and acceptance since the girl had arrived. While not a particularly anxious person, Jill had begun to question the future in a more blatant way. Now it seemed that the answers were coming before she had even contemplated the question. She ascended the stairs to her office with a renewed sense of purpose.

As darkness fell, once again the fog rolled in and the salty smell of the sea permeated the atmosphere.

Chapter 14

Man on a Plane on the Sidewalk

Jack made her way to the sanctuary. In the beginning she referred to her private place as the basement, but as time went on she was impressed with the idea that her room was indeed a private sanctuary.

Across the road from the church a man of small stature took pause on the corner. His mind was consumed with thoughts of his daughter. As he began to continue his journey a sound became louder, so he stopped to see where it might be coming from. It was a beautiful song but intuitively he knew he had never heard it before. In just a moment he realized he was sitting in the rear of a small commercial plane. He was headed to California. It was cold, and the plane sat on the tarmac of LaGuardia Airport not moving. He turned to the woman sitting next to him commenting that it seemed to be taking longer than usual for the plane to prepare for take-off. Soon a flight attendant stood, making a request for several passengers to please disembark due to a weight imbalance on the aircraft. They were offering double fares back and so on, but no one moved. They then began to up the ante with a large monetary bonus, and at that point two people stood up. The woman spoke to the man explaining that she really had to get home due to her job. She had been given the flight as a gift from her daughter to visit New York for her birthday. She then turned to her iPod and began fooling with the dials. Thinking the ordeal was over the man began to relax when another flight attendant stood up requesting a redistribution of the passenger load. The woman glanced his way and smiled stating that it was obvious that they couldn't help the situation due to the fact that they were seated in the last seat of the plane on the left side. There really wasn't anywhere for either of them to go unless it was the rest room. For several moments no one moved. The flight attendant became agitated stating that unless at least two people took seats to the rear, the plane would be grounded for the safety of all the passengers. The man looked forward with anticipation observing some heavier passengers hoping they would take the hint. Finally, a very thin, almost frail looking young woman stood up and made her way to the rear of the plane. The man spoke to her; "Thank you so much for doing that. It showed a lot of consideration." The young girl gave the man a surly look stating, "I just want to get the hell out of here." She then found a seat to the right two rows up from the man and woman. The woman said nothing and soon the plane was in the air. When clearance was given the woman took out her iPod and began scrolling for a movie. She wasn't in any mood to chat with the stern looking man sitting next to her. Unfortunately the man began to question her about the iPod and she responded. The man remembered clearly how excited the woman seemed with her new toy. She began to explain that her daughter always gave her the latest in electronic technology and it had been fun to experiment with it. As their conversation progressed the man was drawn into what the woman was saying. She began to share some of her life and relationship with God. "You know, the Lord has a plan for everyone, and my failures have finally become more of a distant memory to me", she stated. "What do you mean?" the man said. "Well, for a long time I felt like I had failed my daughter, and in fact did to a great degree, but learning about forgiveness and applying it to my life has made all the difference. Do you have a daughter?" she asked. Suddenly the man began to look forward and shake his head pointing down to a napkin that he was writing on. When he finished he handed the napkin to the woman and when she read what it said she understood. He had written, "please don't speak too loud; my daughter is sitting right there, pointing two rows ahead. She's the one who changed seats. I want to hear what you have to say but I don't want her to think that we're talking about *her*." The man then began to write another note. It said "my daughter has severe anorexia and I'm taking her to a special clinic in California. If the treatment doesn't work, then there are no other options. I've had her in every treatment facility available, but she just doesn't respond. I'm so afraid. She could die."

The man remembered the look on the woman's face as compassionate deep and sincere. She said "oh, I understand." After a few minutes had gone by the woman began to speak in a very low tone. "I always thought of myself as a failure. No matter what I did I screwed it up. But then one day I gave my heart to God and something changed. I knew within myself that I could do anything I put my mind to. I started playing the guitar and singing. It was something I had never done before. Then I went back to college and earned my bachelor's degree. Then I wrote a book that was published. Something inside of me believes that nothing is an accident, and you sitting here next to me is a divine appointment." The man remembered telling her that he didn't have any faith, or spiritual life for that matter. Then the woman asked him to write his daughter's name on the napkin promising to pray for her and him. She spoke a little more about fear and how she had lived most of her life battling it. "I was afraid of everything, but no one knew because I would just act out pretending to be brave. Now I don't have to act. I can be me. Jesus is the healer of all our infirmities." The man remembered nodding his head and listening. Soon they arrived at their destination and before leaving the plane the man took the woman's hand and said "thank you, I do believe this was a divine appointment. Please pray for my daughter."

The man opened his eyes, faintly hearing the music and began to walk slowly making his way to the waterfront. There he met his lovely daughter waiting in front of a local Café with a large smile on her face. "Hi daddy! I'm so glad you came to meet me here." It had been two years of recovery and his precious daughter had bloomed. He asked her what finally happened, and she just stared intently into his eyes and said, "I read a book about God and how some people call him Abba Daddy and I thought of you. I felt an enormous rush of love swarm all over me and knew I could do anything with my dad's love!"

Chapter 15

Born in the Month of November

Jack sat with her back against the damp wall. Her guitar lay reposed against the only straight-backed chair in the room. The fire was fading. She wasn't sure if the gas was low, or if it was just her imagination, but the little stove seemed to be running out of fuel. There were no street sounds and it was eerily quiet; just the way she liked it. Her legs felt cold, so she grabbed a light blanket and threw it over her knees. Her legs stretched out before her on the cool cement floor. There was an old Native American type rug thrown down at some time and it looked weathered, tired almost. That was how she felt. Her thoughts ran unclear.

Outside, the fog though light at the moment, was steadily moving onto land. The sea used the humid wetness as a harness over sand covered places where it drifted.

The woman stood motionless as she leaned against the pole facing the church across the street. She was wondering what it would be like to have all of your prizes taken away. It happened all the time in many different ways. Some suffered loss due to no fault of their own.

Maybe an unusually powerful storm raged through and devastated your home taking precious memories with it. Or perhaps, not believing in yourself enough caused you to take a drug to enhance your performance, and in the end, you were found out; now, all of your hard-earned prizes are gone. So what does that leave a person to cling to? Or it could be that a person decided to be the authentic one who lived inside, and self-imposed exposure brought disgust and alienation by the family and friends that you thought you had. Many people are forced to endure such pain when the closet door is opened. Sometimes people are forced into quasi-exile by misunderstanding. What about death? You give your heart away and then must bury it in the deep earth because no one lives forever, and maybe, just maybe you're the one left.

The music began to play.

I believe in God, but when I think about God it's like bee's buzzing around in my head and they're stinging me, and I swat, and I swat to clear a path that doesn't hurt but they won't stop long enough, and I just give up, hoping my allergies to their venom will just kill me so I can stop thinking about god.

My god is too confusing because this god looks like everything that I hate, in myself and in others. What is god telling me, if anything? Stop just stop! Now here is my god giving me good advice. I can't shut up long enough to hear you god, and the buzzing is driving me crazy, especially when I'm alone, and I'm alone a lot. The other day a guy said to his audience, "you need to do one thing, and do you know what that one thing is?" He went on, "get alone with God. I mean you need to spend time alone with God if you ever want to really *know Him*. Ok, I'm thinking, I spend a whole bunch of time alone with myself, and have been presuming that when I pray, God is listening; but maybe my alone time isn't productive because, hey I'm just alone; period. I do question mentally if I know anything anymore regarding my own personal spiritual life. I mean, there's a lot of stuff out there about being authentic and real and taking off the mask, etc. but really, what does it mean? The bible is the trump card in everyone's game of religion, and oh halleluiah, there are as many interpretations as there are people; probably millions, so what's the truth?

Ok, here's a truth. I was born in the month of November; right smack dab in the middle, and I hate to tell people that because they automatically make assumptions about me because they read a lot of astrology which is just cheap entertainment at its best and lies at its worst. I want to tell them I was born in July because those people get a better report regarding their likeable personalities. But when I really think about it I want to be born in December; yeah, December 25th, Jesus birthday. That would give me alignment with someone really significant in history, and then I find out that Jesus wasn't really born then, but probably entered into the world sometime in the spring, like maybe March or April and honestly the few people I've known who had those birthdays really didn't impress me as very spiritual, and now anyone reading this will be offended if hey were born then, so I'm back to being the angry November middle child who is scared and offensive at the same time. My predicament is universal. We all want to be someone else when we get caught at not being our best self. So it's all about outward appearance. I believe I hear music coming from somewhere.......

The church can be such a mean and unforgiving place. Why is that? Do we cling to the past as a refuge from the present? Let's stop hating our parents and realize that they were just like us.; imperfect. Wiping their memory across the mud flat of *shame on them, hooray for me*, is a useless exercise that only belittles other broken people who need to know that God is love. Three simple words put into action can be the catalyst for a renewed life. Wanna know what they are? You have to do it two different ways, and it goes like this: **I forgive you,** and **I forgive myself.**

Remember, God is love I John 4:7-8, is the quintessential description of who God is according to the bible. My bible has a little heading right through to the 16th verse and I like it a lot. It simply says, "seeing God through love". How hard is that? Oh, it's really hard without God. The authentic you must insert the authentic God into your very spirit by acceptance of this basic truth about Him. The truth about you is that you don't know Him if you have not experienced this one fundamental truth about the nature of God. This is why the church keeps people out who they deem worthless. They may be calling themselves the church, but in the end, they will be told that He never knew them if love isn't the engine driving the machine.

The woman leaned against the light pole feeling depleted and energized at the same time. The buzzing had stopped. The bees were gone. Only the sound of beautiful music filled her head.

Chapter 16

Woman on the Sidewalk

We are standing on holy ground, and I can feel the touch of angels all around...the words were clear in her mind as she stood, almost incoherent on the street corner. It was as if an invisible cord was holding her hostage and there was a distant sound. Something quiet, streaming through her body and no earthly description could hold the thought. "I'm more than lost", her thoughts were beaming through her thoughtless mind.

Jack felt the distant thunder that sometimes clued her mind to just be quiet. It clapped the loud eternal sound beckoning her retreat to listen, and not respond.

The monster had entered the room and she must be quiet. A five-year-old child, I sit and wonder if mommy will be mad if I pee on her again. All these years I've wandered not knowing where the road would lead and now, here I am in this dusky town waiting for the end. How I wish it would end, but there are others to consider.

The not-so-young woman was alone. Here she thinks about the rescue of her life, and how it all came about.

A leaf fell from a tree slowly cascading downward

until it had swayed toward her limp hand hanging at her side. She turned her palm upward to catch the dying thing, thinking it looked a lot like her own life. But the wind caught it suddenly and it flew upward again, out of sight. "That is a lot like me", she thought.

"Where are you going?" a voice spoke. The woman looked around but did not see anyone. She returned to her thoughts.

The voice spoke again, "you are standing on Holy ground." "What?" the woman questioned. The voice did not answer, so the woman began to speak to herself.

"I did not do anything on purpose to hurt anyone intentionally", the woman spoke out loud to no-one in particular. "Oh really?" an inner voice responded. "What about the question your own daughter asked you?" the voice went on.

The woman remembered the conversation. The twelve-year-old had just returned from visiting her grandmother who lived 2 thousand miles away. "I don't want to visit her anymore" the child said. "What did she say?" the woman asked. There was a pause, and the girl quickly stated; "because she asked me if it was awful having a mother who was a Lesbian." The woman looked at the joy of her life and felt a stabbing pain once again. She could not remember what her response was and was just now recalling the long-ago conversation. She did remember her daughter said she related the conversation to her dad and told him she did not want to go to the woman's house again. "Such pain "was all the woman could think at the moment. Her mind then went to another time and place. She was riding in the car with her boyfriend at the time. He had been insistent on having sex, but she was reluctant. She began to tell him why. It had to do with a childhood molestation and suddenly the boyfriend said, "oh god, not another girl molested by an adult male", and so she had ended the conversation and dug a deeper hole to place the shame. The perpetrator was her own father. Then she recalled that very same night her father had beaten her mother at a gas station and thrown her on the ground bleeding and crying. He had crushed her jaw and blood was flowing like a red river all over her face. Then he got in the car and told her two brother's and herself to shut up our crying and began to drive away. He molested her that night after they got home, and the details became a blur over the years. It was to become her unvisited place as she grew up, and for many years the rage and anger surfaced in every relationship she attempted. The door to recovery would not open until another woman befriended her. Her thoughts were no longer her own and she felt the pull of the music taming the emotions that had lain dormant for so many years.

The hardened shell remained and only music or comedy could soften the response that was inevitable when such a subject was approached.

Like a raging storm, the woman ran away and never came home again. Her life was distant to anyone who tried to be a friend. Only a select few were allowed the entrance to her heart and even then, it was conditional. Her thoughts came like a straight wind arrowed to beat her through the storm that was internalized with such disdain. She remembered the violence against the flesh that bore her into the world, a weak, sickly child who cried all the time. The empty place stayed that way for most of her life, until the day she was once again thrown away, like the trash a filthy rag not fit to be alive and serve another day. Then, another whisper of a human saw the truth in her and showed a desire to be a friend, and it was like holding on in the dark when she said yes, let me be yours, for I am nothing, disappearing before the eyes of those she trusted most, I will dare to take a chance and give you what I have. And now in retrospect she knows that it was a crumb, barely visible and only another naked eye could see the truth. Need stood out like a neon sign, but she was oblivious to it. The new love was as broken, even more, than she could ever know, and when they became as one it was like being brand new and the normalcy of living for the day became her daily prayer.

"Sex is the greatest lie" her thoughts once again began to internalize, and whoever she was supposed to be would never happen, and she knew it, because all hope had been crushed under foot by any who tried to define her. It was impossible to describe what you never endured yourself let alone what you had personally known in the flesh. Who can know what grace means when being hard is the only defense you have to survive? Is healing possible? Does being set free mean you will never struggle or feign the blows the fist aims at you, or does the life you want to live only start on the other side of the grave?

The girl saw the crushing blow hit the mother who gave her life and she saw her hit the ground crumbling like a broken twig, and she cried, and cried, "don't leave her there!". She saw the body thrown out of a car driving down the road, her beautiful head of hair torn as he flung her out the door, the car still moving, and she cried again, "don't leave her there, don't leave her!", because she knew she would never see her again, because she would be dead.

But she didn't die, not then, not physically. It took time for the full revelation to take root and she became what she knew she was never meant to be, and the result was, I became who I never thought I'd be.

I am standing on holy ground, and I can hear the brush of angel's wings all around....

Chapter 17

Man on the Sidewalk

Their cars were hiding under the limbs of a great tree, and the talk began.

Sometimes I feel like I'm looking through the wrong set of glasses. It's as if I accidentally picked up someone else's eyewear and the lens is distorting everything that I look at. I know something's wrong but fail to just reach up and remove them. Or perhaps I went to the eye doctor for an exam and he was determined that everyone he examined that day would be near-sighted and just fit them all with the lenses that suited his mood, and not what they really needed. This is how I sometimes see the church.

No matter where you go it seems they all have an agenda, no matter what the individuals in the congregation need. The powers that be give the same prescription to everyone; one size fits all. I think they may teach this ideology in seminary. "For all have sinned…and come short of the glory of God." (paraphrase-Romans 3:23). So all have the same problem and it stands to reason that the solution to that problem would be a universal antidote. "But wait", I hear the announcer say, buy one at this low price and we'll throw in an additional two more items to give to all your friends. You better hurry though because this is a limited time, limited choice offer and we only have a few left!" I can feel myself getting anxious and start to respond hurriedly so as not to miss out on this great deal. After all, every household needs this.

My young friend stood motionless, with a kind of grief hanging from his emotionless eyes. His words were few. "I can't tell you exactly what happened because things are still in process, so to speak." He went on, "I spent my 40th birthday in jail. I still can't believe it but that's what happened."

My response was simple. "I know" I said. The truth was, someone had told me what they read in the paper, and it really bothered me. My friend went on to say that the church he attended had notified him that he was no longer welcome there, and this included his family. Actually, one family member was told they could stay but could no longer participate in the choir or anything else for that matter. He wasn't actually told this in person. He received an email to that effect. So of course he never went back.

"I didn't know there was so much hate" he said. I wasn't sure what he was being accused of and frankly told him that at this time it didn't seem to matter much to me, because I wanted to impart some unconditional love that the Lord had shown me. "Thank you" was all he said. I then gave him some gas money for his vehicle because he told me he was destitute.

The music drifted across the road and the man fell into the rhythm of what was being played while remembering the conversation.

Chapter 18

Woman and Jesus on the Sidewalk

"Music acts like a magic key, to which the most tightly closed heart opens." Maria Von Trapp

The sound of Bob Dylan declaring "it aint me babe" blared through the am radio in my 1957 Chevy while I drove to my temporary home from my temporary job. I love that song. For some reason that radio station played that particular song every night at just about the time I was crossing the railroad tracks that lead to the room in the house where I was staying. My soul cried along with the lyrics and became my mantra. It surely wasn't me. I didn't know who *me* was. And now, walking through the little town in Oregon made me want to hear it again. The darkness had fallen and thrown an eerie glow on the buildings lining the sidewalk. The solitude was remarkably noisy. A song began from somewhere and with every step I felt its promise. An inner prayer had begun once again. I never know how to begin my prayers. Should I say something like, Dear God, or just begin rambling. Music seemed to be the key that for me, unlocked the river of dialogue between myself and my unseen companion. Thoughts would come more as questions, such as, am I doing this right? Should I bow down, or fall prostrate on my face in the dirt to show homage to my creator? I don't know anymore. I've read about saints of old who did all kinds of things to get Gods attention. Bodily torture was really popular at one time but that just didn't make sense to me. We were created in God's image, so wouldn't it be sacrilege to harm the very vessel that He ordained for His purpose? There are so many questions and yet just one answer; or so they say.

Jack had begun to play. The sound resonated out into what seemed infinity. The woman stood silently listening and then had a vision. It appeared that millions of pieces of refuse were falling from the sky, appearing like snow, only black. She felt overwhelmed. There was so much that the very air became full of these tiny particles and worst of all was the cacophony of anguished sound. Her heart cried out, "oh Lord help me!" My sorrow is too great to bear. Not only did the woman see her own sins, but she was enduring the sins of others. Every once in a while, she would see a particular wrong that she had done and would become grieved almost unto death. And then she just fell weakly to the ground with the thought that this had all been taken care of and she no longer needed to see or feel it again.

"Can you hear me?" a voice gently spoke. "yes" she answered. The voice went on. "You torture yourself needlessly. I am caring for every hurt at all times and yet you do not believe fully. Here, take my hand." The woman reached into what appeared to be nothingness and then felt something firm around her fingers. "What do you see now?" the voice asked. The woman thought for a moment and realized she was looking at an enormous cross that literally filled the entire sky. Even though it was nightfall there was a light all around and she had the urge to fly, if only she could. The anguish disappeared, and she felt peace beyond description. Her first impulse was to ask what she needed to do and instantly her hand felt a squeeze and the thought went no further. Her teeth had become clenched and she now realized that her jaw was slack, and a faint smile had appeared upon her mouth. She then spoke. "I've always been afraid of you. Anytime I got lost it made me want to run." "I know" the voice spoke quietly. "I've felt alone for so long" the woman said. "Yes, I know" the voice replied. The voice went on, "I have loved you with a never-ending love, and now you know and must keep this promise in your heart at all times. Never let another take it away. See, the sky is clear, and the road is paved just for you. Now walk assured that you are held tightly by love and not restraint."

The woman opened her eyes and heard a very distant song so sweetly that she could almost taste it.

Chapter 19

Jack Departs

A thunderous clap sounded above Jack's head and she jerked awake with a start. It was time to go. After last night she knew in her heart that she must be moving on. "I will go and say goodbye to Jill" she thought and then be on my way. Her eyes focused downward to her bare feet and then to the corner where her worn boots were sitting. She dressed slowly, inwardly hoping for the chance to stay just a little longer. It was not to be. After dressing and attaching her backpack she wrapped her fingers around the handle of the guitar case and headed out.

Jill had just emerged from her car and was heading for the church doors when she caught a glimpse of Jack walking up the street in her direction. Jill felt sadness but also knew that the girl's time in the community had been beneficial. She could not actually name anything specific that the girl had done other than use the room she had made available, however, the atmosphere felt lighter and more hopeful than she could ever remember.

The two met as Jack approached the corner where

the church seemed to sit in repose. "Good morning" Jill cheerfully announced. Jack murmured a quiet response and immediately began to speak about her upcoming departure. Jill reacted with a smile stating that she knew the day would come, but that she was so very pleased to have met the young girl and began to wish her well in the future. Jack reached into her jacket pocket and retrieved the key. Holding it in a somewhat clenched fist she slowly opened her palm extending her hand toward the pastor and in a soft tone said, "thank you". "No, thank you" Jill responded. The pastor did not feel the need to question the girl any further about her future plans but did ask if she would please come inside for coffee and breakfast. "That would be nice" Jack said.

After preparing the coffee and rolls Jill turned and said there was something else she wanted to give the girl. "I really don't need anything" Jack said, but then noticed a carafe of wine and a small loaf of bread sitting on the sideboard of the makeshift counter. Jill went on. "I would like to partake of communion with you Jack, if it's alright with you." Jack felt a small thrill run through her as she nodded her head indicating it would be more than fine. A smile emerged from Jack's face, such as she had never displayed before and shortly Jill picked up the elements bringing them to the small table where Jack was sitting.

After their communion together Jill had the distinct feeling that she had experienced something akin to having had her feet washed in a clear pool making her lighter in spirit and thought.

Jack was now exiting the side door of the church for

the last time and Jill stood just within the framework gazing at what began to appear as an apparition. The sun suddenly broke through the thick layer of clouds that seemed to always adorn the little town this time of year. The pastor stood gazing above with no thought other than the fact that she had no doubt about the creator and His personal touch as she still felt the Eucharist flowing through her body. She looked again to see the girl, but a light mist had replaced where Jack had been standing just a moment ago.

Epilogue

My thanks go out to anyone who took the time to read this tale of perhaps the forgotten and misunderstood people who, earnestly desire to personally know their creator. I believe the grace of God is evidenced by the creator himself, in allowing fallen humans to nail Jesus, the Son of God to the cross, thus bringing evidence of our Father's most profound love for everyone.

My prayer is that the reader would find peace as promised by Christ, through these characters, and perhaps be able to hear His gentle voice and calm assurance that no matter what might have befallen you, the lover of your soul came to bring you into His compassionate love while on earth, and in the life to come.

May you enjoy His companionship as His beloved child.

Remember that when someone doesn't accept you as you are, it is their imperfection of non-acceptance that is wrong; God made you perfect.

Mercy comes from the hand of God, and he releases the gift to us in the form of understanding, *i.e.* compassion.

Printed in the United States
By Bookmasters